D0891695

A SAGE PROFESSIONAL PAPER

WILLIAM T. DALY

The Revolutionary:
A Review and Synthesis

COMPARATIVE POLITICS SERIES

Editors: HARRY ECKSTEIN and TED ROBERT GURR

Series Number: 01-025   Volume 3

The Revolutionary:
A Review and Synthesis

WILLIAM T. DALY
Stockton State College

 SAGE PUBLICATIONS / Beverly Hills   London

For information address:

SAGE PUBLICATIONS, INC. SAGE PUBLICATIONS LTD
275 South Beverly Drive St George's House / 44 Hatton Garden
Beverly Hills, California 90212 London E C 1

International Standard Book Number 0-8039-0143-7

Library of Congress Catalog Card No. 72-77747

FIRST PRINTING

CONTENTS

The Revolutionary:
A Review and Synthesis

WILLIAM T. DALY
Stockton State College

The significance of revolutions and the men who make them as a subject of study hardly needs to be argued. Even if the term revolution is defined—as it will be here—to include only those attempts to impose, by any means necessary, a rapid and comprehensive change not only in the way the members of a society behave but also in the way they think—still the emergence of communism, fascism, and anticolonial nationalism has meant that the world has been virtually awash in this type of revolution since World War I. Even American domestic politics now contains increasingly vocal groups which view revolution, in this most extreme sense of the word, as a legitimate form of political action.[1]

As a result, the search for patterns of revolutionary politics, which will make the course of revolutionary activity more predictable, and its usefulness as a means of social change more calculable, is of significance to political activists as well as to academics—whether their focus is foreign or domestic and whether their commitment is to the maintenance of the status quo or to its destruction. This study will seek to describe and explain such patterns in the political behavior of revolutionaries—the leaders and hard-core operatives of revolutionary movements.

But if it is easy to justify the study of revolutions and revolutionaries in terms of the significance of the subject, such a study cannot be justified by the standard observation that this significant area has been neglected by scholars. Precisely because of the centrality of revolution in twentieth-century politics, the literature on the subject is already substantial. As a result, any reexamination of the subject must begin with an attempt to extract and synthesize the useful materials from the work that has already been done. This study will be confined to that preliminary task.

Specifically, I will argue (1) that a review of the existing descriptions of revolutionary politics indicates a good deal of tacit agreement on the distinctive characteristics of revolutionaries, i.e., on those patterns of political behavior shared by revolutionaries but not by nonrevolutionaries, and (2) that a review of the conflicting explanations of revolutionary politics indicates the usefulness of focusing, for purposes of explanation, on the personal ordeal which revolution imposes on the leaders and hard-core operatives who make it.

It should be noted explicitly at this point that such a review and synthesis necessarily involves a process of selection, which may result in an incomplete picture of the relevant literature, considered as a whole, and a process of evaluation, which may result in an incomplete picture of the individual works which are selected, considered as integrated wholes.

The works selected for review were confined to those which were (1) theoretical or comparative treatments of revolution or revolutionaries—because of the desire to maximize the relevance of the works selected to my concerns and hence minimize the damage done to the author's intent in extracting that relevance, (2) contemporary, in the sense of having been written since the Bolshevik revolution—because of the discovery that most of the relevant material in earlier works had already been incorporated into more recent works, and (3) influential, in terms of their apparent impact on other analysts—because of the desire to objectify, albeit loosely, the subjective standards of quality which are an inevitable part of such a selection process. Thus what follows is offered only as a reasonably comprehensive review of contemporary and influential theoretical treatments of revolution, and not as a comprehensive review of all the works which treat the subject of revolution.

The selected works were, of course, evaluated in terms of their contribution to the central concern of this paper—the description and explanation of the patterns of political behavior peculiar to revolutionaries. Since this was not always the central concern of the authors, their work is sometimes criticized and praised for characteristics which were not central to their purposes. Thus, what follows is offered only as a reasonably just evaluation of the contribution of these works to the description and explanation of revolutionary behavior, and not as a just evaluation of their total worth.

DESCRIPTIONS

The idea that individuals who conform to our definition of revolutionaries are bound together by certain ways of thinking and behaving which set them apart from nonrevolutionaries is not new. The emergence of fascism after World War I and its attacks on, and differences from, both democracy and traditional autocracy, imposed on the policies of powerful states a distinctive pattern of political behavior not easily described within those traditional categories. And the discovery of some similarities between fascism and Stalinist communism replaced the view of fascism as an aberration with the suspicion that those distinctive patterns of political behavior might be shared by a number of movements and regimes across ideological lines. The result was a series of attempts to find comparable patterns of behavior in other movements and regimes and, on the basis of that comparison, to delineate the central characteristics of this seemingly new political phenomenon. The results of this search for the central characteristics of what we have called the revolutionary have, however, varied, because of variations in the focus of the analysts. As a result, the portrait of the revolutionary presented here will be a composite—constructed from images of the revolutionary as mad man, as mass man, as political man, and as revolutionary man.

MAD MAN

The students of "psychopathology" in politics focus on periods of breakdown in established social or individual norms and see the revolutionary as mad man—in the sense that they see, as his central distinguishing characteristic, a particular, distorted view of reality.

This group is in fact composed of two subgroups who use different sets of concepts to describe the revolutionary. The first group sees revolutionary behavior as only one form of "collective behavior," i.e., those behavior patterns which appear when large numbers of individuals reject established social norms. As a result, they ground their description of revolutionary behavior empirically in the initial stages of an extremely wide range of movements which includes, in addition to the major revolutionary movements not only other less political attempts to totally remake men, such as the militant stages of the major religions, nativist cults among primitive peoples, and communitarian withdrawal movements, but also a wide variety of movements more limited in their duration and in the scope of their intentions, such as mob actions, financial and physical panics, and fads. The second group sees revolutionary behavior as only one form of individual neurosis, i.e., individual behavior contrary to established social norms, and grounds their description of the revolutionary empirically either in fascism—viewed as being the most clearly neurotic of the revolutionary movements—or in the study of individual revolutionary leaders.

But in spite of the fact that these works examine a large number of different individuals and movements widely scattered over space and time, and examine them with two different sets of concepts, the descriptions of the revolutionary which emerge are remarkably similar. The central distinguishing characteristic of the revolutionary is viewed as being his dichotomous view of reality, which divides the world into opposing forces of absolute good and absolute evil, rejects the possibility of any middle ground between the two, and derives from that world view a highly simplified set of guidelines for behavior.

(1) The complex and unintegrated set of beliefs about causality which serve the nonrevolutionary as guidelines for effective behavior are replaced by a tendency to see the cause of all problems, no matter how diverse and logically unrelated, in a single force for evil and to see the solution of all those problems in a single force for good.

(2) The complex and unintegrated values which serve the nonrevolutionary as guidelines for moral behavior are replaced by a tendency to view as moral any behavior which contributes to the victory of the forces of good over the forces of evil and to view as immoral any behavior which delays or endangers that victory.

(3) The willingness of the nonrevolutionary to act without explicit reference to his beliefs and values, and hence to act in accordance with different and often contradictory sets of those guidelines in different areas of his life, is replaced by a tendency to insist that all behavior conform strictly and explicitly to the new and highly simplified set of beliefs and values. [2]

But the rejection of established social norms not only results in rigid adherence to a highly simplified new set of norms, it also results in a frantic drive for the approval of that adherence by others. Such, at least, is the argument of the students of "mass society."

MASS MAN

The students of "mass society" focus both on periods of initial breakdown in established social norms and on the earlier stages of the movements which grow out of that breakdown, and see the revolutionary as mass man—in the sense that they see, as his central distinguishing characteristic, the glorification of, and identification with, the masses.

This view of the revolutionary is grounded empirically in the study of the earlier stages of German and Italian fascism—conspicuous among revolutionary movements because of their commitment and ability to mobilize mass enthusiasm—and to a lesser degree in the study of Bolshevism. It describes the revolutionary as being, above all, a mass man in three respects:

(1) He goes beyond the view, generally accepted since the French Revolution even by nonrevolutionaries, that political power must be rooted in some degree of mass support, toward viewing the emancipated masses as a key to omnipotence—giving the man who has their support the physical ability to overcome all obstacles.

(2) He goes beyond the generally accepted view that political legitimacy must be rooted in some degree of mass support, toward viewing the emancipated masses as a key to virtue—giving the man who has their support the moral right to violate all other canons of morality.

(3) He goes beyond the generally accepted practice of claiming and pursuing mass support, toward the pursuit of enthusiastic and unanimous mass support and the destruction of alternative foci of mass attention and loyalty which might divert some of that mass emotion from himself. [3]

But once the revolutionary has consolidated power, both this commitment to the masses and his commitment to his new beliefs and values give way before the emergence of another more ominous half of the revolutionary character. Such, at least, is the argument of the students of "totalitarianism."

POLITICAL MAN

The students of totalitarianism focus on the revolutionary come to power and see him as political man—in the sense that they see, as his central distinguishing characteristic, a ruthless pursuit of absolute power.

Whereas many of the works on the revolutionary as mad man and as mass man focused on movements which never came to power or on the early period of the revolutionary in power, the works on totalitarianism focus on the revolutionary once he has consolidated his hold on the power of the state and begun the task of remaking men and societies. As a result, the picture of the revolutionary as political man is grounded empirically in the study of the major contemporary revolutionary regimes—Fascist Italy, Nazi Germany, Soviet (and in particular Stalinist) Russia, and to a lesser degree, Communist China. [4]

That picture of the revolutionary come to power is one of internal conflict and contradiction—of the continuation and formalization of the characteristics of mad man and mass man, but now coexisting with and conflicting with a ruthless pursuit of power.

The dichotomous world view and highly simplified beliefs and values discovered by those who saw the revolutionary as mad man are continued and formalized, according to the students of totalitarianism, as a *dogmatic ideology* with three elements:

(1) The highly simplified beliefs, which related all events either to a single force for good or to a single force for evil, are formalized as a set of deterministic laws which govern the course of the struggle between those forces and assure predictability in the short run and victory for the forces of good in the long run.

(2) The highly simplified values, which judged the morality of all actions solely in terms of their contribution to the victory of the forces for good, are formalized as a utopia, toward which the deterministic laws are inexorably moving and in behalf of which any actions are morally justified.

(3) The insistence that all behavior conform explicitly and strictly to those highly simplified beliefs and values is formalized in the revolutionary's attempts to achieve complete identification with the ideology—by elaborate arguments to prove that all his actions are logically derived from the laws of the ideology (and hence contribute to the realization of the utopia) and by rewriting history, or actually remaking the reality upon which history will be based, to make his infallible interpretation of those laws a visible fact.[5]

And just as the students of totalitarianism see the highly simplified beliefs and values—discovered by those who saw the revolutionary as mad man—continued and formalized as ideological dogmatism, so too do they see the glorification of and identification with the masses—discovered by those who saw the revolutionary as mass man—continued and formalized as an institutionalized *populism*. The students of totalitarianism give little emphasis to the first two characteristics emphasized by those who saw the revolutionary as mass man—the tendency to view the emancipated masses as the key to (1) omnipotence, and (2) virtue—because, as we shall see in the section on explanation, they do not believe in the sincerity of the revolutionary's protestations to this effect. But most of these analysts do concede the continuation of these two characteristics after the consolidation of power at least to the degree of confessing that the revolutionary does seem to see political power and legitimacy as being rooted in the masses to such a degree that he probably has more in common with the democratic political leader than with the traditional autocrat. And almost all the students of totalitarianism emphasize the continuation and formalization of the third characteristic of the revolutionary as mass man—the attempt to identify with the masses by pursuing enthusiastic and unanimous mass support. Whatever their doubts about his motivations, in terms of his visible behavior the revolutionary is seen as pursuing complete identification with the masses—in the sense that he rejects by logical argument all traditional distinctions between rulers and ruled, between state and society, and in the sense that he attempts to make that complete identification a visible fact, by destroying all groups independent of the movement which might divert mass loyalties and energies, by insisting on the active involvement of all individuals in regime-sponsored activities, and by staging periodic mass demonstrations of enthusiastic and unanimous support.[6]

But coexisting with this dogmatism and populism, the students of totalitarianism discern another, and increasingly dominant, side of the revolutionary—a ruthless pursuit of power which develops into the polar opposites of dogmatism and populism, into cynicism and elitism.

Although, as noted above, the students of totalitarianism find in the behavior of the revolutionary evidence of a dogmatism more extreme than that of the most principled of nonrevolutionary political leaders, they also find evidence of a power-oriented *cynicism* extreme enough to embarrass the most opportunistic of nonrevolutionary political leaders—not only with respect to the principles of the prerevolutionary order but also with respect to the principles enshrined in the revolutionary's own ideology.

(1) Thus although the revolutionary pictures himself as walking in lockstep with deterministic laws of history, he also seems capable of a voluntarism which rejects all limitations on what he can do, including those implied by the laws of his own ideology, and which results in policy shifts which are breathtaking in their scope and frequency.

(2) Similarly, although the revolutionary meticulously justifies all his actions as contributing to the realization of the ideology's utopia, he also seems capable of an instrumentalism which rejects all moral limitations on what he may do, including those implied by the utopia of his own ideology, which judges the morality of actions and men solely in terms of their contribution to the power of the movement, and which often results in the creation of the counter-utopia, i.e., of conditions precisely the opposite of those which were to prevail in the utopia.[7]

The picture is similar with respect to *elitism*. Although, as noted above, the students of totalitarianism find in the behavior of the revolutionary evidence of a populism more extreme than that of the most democratic nonrevolutionary political leaders, they also find evidence of a power-oriented elitism which exceeds that of the most despotic traditional autocrat, in terms of the scope and centralization of the imposed controls.

(1) Thus although the revolutionary sees in the emancipation of the masses from repression and passivity the key to irresistible political power, he stifles all possibility for such spontaneous support by a set of controls which are comprehensive in scope (from which the term "totalitarianism" is derived)—in the sense that they involve not only the attempt to destroy all organized opposition, international as well as domestic, but also the attempt to control all social relationships that might provide the basis for opposition, and, hence, to control the daily lives of the passive masses.

(2) Similarly, although the revolutionary apparently sees the emancipated masses as the ultimate arbiters of virtue, he centralizes those comprehensive controls in the hands of a small number of men deemed to be the only ones virtuous enough to be trusted with them. He excludes all others from the circle of trust and power—not only his active political opposition but also the passive masses and those active sympathizers who for one reason or another refuse to accept the absolute discipline required of members of the movement. And even within the movement, all who openly question leadership policy, and even those who are guilty only of having served the movement faithfully so long that they are suspected of being weary and no longer reliable, are regularly purged or at least pushed away from the levers of power, until the leader achieves, according to the students of totalitarianism, the closest thing to true one-man rule that history has ever seen. The final and most bizarre element in this pattern of centralization is the leveling, against all those who have been excluded in this fashion from the circle of trust and power, of a terroristic violence—which differs from other forms of political violence in that the selection of targets often seems to be unrelated to oppositional activity or even to any calculation of the potential for opposition, in that it is directed against a continuous and seemingly endless series of enemies, and in that it brings to bear on those enemies a level of brutality which belies any sense of shared humanity between the revolutionary and the enemy.[8]

Thus the image of the revolutionary as political man is a perplexing combination of a zealot saint and a power-hungry butcher. For he is in some respects more dogmatic and populistic than the most idealistic of democratic political leaders and, in others, more cynical and elitist than the most ruthless of traditional despots. (For a summary of this description, see Figure 1).

But even this most detailed and synthetic of descriptions remains incomplete. It is only a snapshot picture of the revolutionary—freezing him at the peak of militant behavior and ignoring variations in the patterns of his behavior as the revolution progresses. Such, at least, is the argument of those who might be called "sociologists of revolution."

REVOLUTIONARY MAN

The sociologists of revolution focus primarily on historical revolutions which have already run full term and see the revolutionary as revolutionary man—in the sense that they see all the distinguishing characteristics described above as only one stage in the larger process of remaking a society.

While some of the more recent works in this group treat contemporary Communist and Nationalist revolutions, most of the sociologies of revolution are grounded empirically in the French, Russian, American, or English (Puritan) revolutions, with some additional reference to such movements as the early militant phases of the major religions, the Reformation, the European revolutions of 1830 and 1848, and a variety of nativist revolts among non-Western peoples under the impact of the West.[9]

If the term *militance* can be used as a general designation for the patterns of dogmatism-cynicism and populism-elitism described above, then the contribution of the sociologists of revolution to our picture of the revolutionary can be summarized by saying that their broad historical perspective has led them to reject both the implication that militant behavior is a very temporary outburst of individual or mass insanity (implied by the psychopathologists and the students of mass society) and the implication that it is a new and permanent form of government (implied by the students of totalitarianism). Instead, while their description of the revolutionary during the most militant stage of the revolution conforms to and reinforces the description of revolutionary behavior constructed up to this point, they argue that the markedness of this pattern of behavior waxes and wanes as the process of remaking a society progresses. And in spite of some differences in terminology, there is a remarkable unanimity on the stages of that process after the collapse of the old order:

(1) Rule by the Moderates—during which the characteristics we have called militance are muted by the dominance of men who prefer limited ends and gentlemanly means to the utopian ends and willingness to use any means, reflected in dogmatism-cynicism, and

who prefer some form of pluralism to the mobilization of the entire populace behind a single tiny elite, reflected in populism-elitism.

(2) Rule by the radicals and terror—during which the full panoply of the characteristics we have called militance develops with the rise to dominance of men committed to rapid and comprehensive change by any means necessary.

(3) Thermidor—which begins as soon as the movement has defeated its organized opposition and restored some modicum of order and during which militance declines and nonrevolutionary patterns of political behavior reemerge.[10]

But while the first two stages of this progression are relatively noncontroversial, one of the few clear-cut differences of opinion in the descriptive literature does emerge with respect to stage three, and with it, the necessity for evaluating the relative plausibility of the two conflicting descriptions. The students of totalitarianism see a sharp increase in militance at precisely the point where the sociologists of revolution see a sharp decline—at the point where the movement has defeated its organized opposition and restored order.

There appears to be an element of plausibility in both these descriptions. On the one hand, militance does appear to increase rather than decrease at this point. The belief to the contrary on the part of the sociologists of revolution appears to have been the result of (1) focusing too much on revolutions in which the leadership never was committed to the rapid and comprehensive remaking of men's minds and behavior (i.e., the American Revolution) or in which the elements of the leadership with such a commitment were removed early (i.e., with the death of Cromwell in the English Revolution and of Robespierre in the French), and (2) the tendency to implicitly view dogmatism and populism as somehow more "revolutionary" than cynicism and elitism and hence to view the growing importance of the latter two as signaling the end of the revolution. But if one considers cynicism and elitism to be as much a part of militance as dogmatism and populism (as indeed the sociologists of revolution themselves frequently do), and if one focuses on revolutions where the members of the original militant leadership remain in power for something approaching a full generation, then the students of totalitarianism appear to be right in asserting that the behavior of such leaders as Stalin after 1928, Hitler after 1934, and Mao after 1956 indicates a mystifying tendency for militance to increase dramatically at precisely that point when the elimination of organized opposition and the restoration of order might seem to have eliminated the need for it. Perhaps the most persuasive evidence of the existence of this additional stage of sharply increased militance after the consolidation of power is the difficulty encountered by the sociologists of revolution in applying their three stage model to Bolshevism—the only one of their major case studies in which members of the original militant leadership remained in power for a protracted period.[11]

On the other hand, the assertion of the sociologists of revolution that militance is only a stage in the revolutionary process and will eventually taper off into more conventional patterns of political behavior seems more in accordance with the facts than the prediction that militance will be institutionalized indefinitely in the form of totalitarian government. Perhaps the most persuasive evidence of this is the degree to which the students of totalitarianism have had to alter their initial predictions of perpetual militance in light of the post-Stalinist decline of militance in Bolshevism—the only one of their major case studies which has survived for a protracted period. Moreover, that evolution seems to indicate not only that militance does eventually decline but also, as the English and French revolutions had already suggested, that the decline might be connected with the demise of the original revolutionary leadership, whether that demise results from the guillotine or from simple human mortality and the succession of generations.[12]

Thus the evidence available in the descriptive literature (admittedly very thin in spots) indicates four stages in the life cycle of those revolutionary movements in which power is retained by members of the original militant leadership:

(1) the muted militance of the reformer,
(2) the full pattern of militant behavior characteristic of the revolutionary,
(3) a sharp increase in militance after the movement has defeated its organized opposition and restored order, and
(4) a tapering off of the militance and the reemergence of nonrevolutionary patterns of political behavior when the men who made the revolution are displaced.

A SYNTHETIC DESCRIPTION

As a result of the similarity, or at least complementarity, of the descriptions contained in the literature, much of the work of creating a synthetic description has already been done simply by reviewing existing descriptions. The synthetic description which emerges from that review need not, of course, be accepted as accurate simply because it appears in the literature. But the fact that so many students of the subject have

Ideological Dogmatism	*Cynicism*
(1) Deterministic laws	(1) Voluntarism
(2) Utopia	(2) Instrumentalism —Counterutopia
(3) Complete identification with ideology —Logically —Factually	

Populism	*Elitism*
(1) Emancipated masses as key to unlimited power	(1) Comprehensive control —Over organized opposition —Over daily lives of masses

(2) Emancipated masses as key to ultimate morality	(2) Centralized control
	—Exclusion of passive masses
	—Exclusion of active sympathizer
	—Exclusion within the movement
	    —of opponents
	    —of the faithful but weary
	    —of all but the leader
	—Terror against the excluded
	    —noncalculable violence
	    —continuous violence
	    —brutal violence

(3) Complete identification with masses —Logically —Factually	

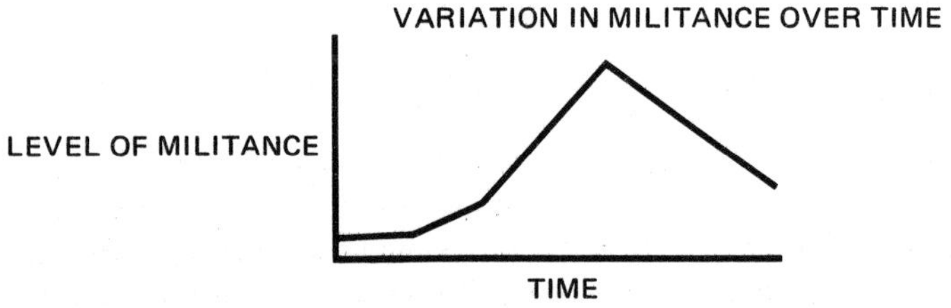

VARIATION IN MILITANCE OVER TIME

LEVEL OF MILITANCE

TIME

Figure 1: ELEMENTS OF MILITANCE

constructed similar or complementary descriptions of the revolution-ary—in spite of the fact that they were using a wide variety of conceptual frameworks to study a wide variety of revolutionaries—does lend some initial plausibility to such a synthetic description.

The picture of the revolutionary which emerges from such a synthesis is not so much the picture of a qualitatively different kind of political leader as it is a picture of the political leader writ large. All political leaders since the advent of mass politics have to some degree combined ideology with pragmatism and mass appeal with elitist practice. The distinctive charac-teristic of the revolutionary is that he apparently combines extreme dogmatism with extreme cynicism and extreme populism with extreme elitism—that he appears to be a genuine combination of zealot saint and power-hungry butcher. The details of that combination, already delineated above, and the variation in the markedness of that combination over time, might be summarized diagramatically as follows.

EXPLANATIONS

There is a good deal less consensus on the explanation of revolutionary behavior than there is on the description of it. As a result, this section will involve a good deal of selection as well as synthesis. Specifically it will involve the attempt to extract and synthesize the strengths, while avoiding the weaknesses, of theories which explain revolutionary behavior in terms of unique factors, situational necessity, familiar motivations, psychological void, and psychological conflict.

UNIQUE FACTORS

The characteristics which we have called militance have often been explained individually and collectively as the result of factors unique to the context of the particular revolutions in which they have appeared. For example, the centralization of power in the Bolshevik movement has been variously explained in terms of the despotic history and character of the Russian people, in terms of the organizational necessities imposed by tsarist repression, and in terms of the necessities imposed by the attempt to remake a technologically backward society in the image of a modernizing Communist ideology.

This type of theory is, of course, useful for explaining the multiform differences which separate revolutions because of the different contexts in which they developed. But its usefulness is limited for our purposes because of its inability to explain the striking similarities in revolutionary behavior (i.e., the characteristics of militance) which seem to appear in spite of enormous differences in local context, and which cannot therefore be easily explained in terms of that context. This is true particularly inasmuch as those similarities appear in spite of differences in history and character as great as those which separate the French from the Chinese, differences in political context as great as those which separate Weimar democracy from tsarist autocracy, differences in levels of technology as great as those which separate New Guinea from Germany, and differences in ideology as great as those which separate liberalism, from communism, from fascism, from anticolonial nationalism.

It is these strikingly similar patterns of behavior which have led many analysts to go beyond explaining the differences among revolutions, in terms of unique causal factors, in the direction of explaining their shared characteristics as well, in terms of shared causal factors. One of the shared causal factors most often noted might be called "situational necessity."

SITUATIONAL NECESSITY

Most of the analysts which were referred to in the descriptive section as "sociologists of revolution" explain militance in terms of situational necessity. That is to say that they accept the necessity of explaining the shared and distinctive behavior patterns of revolutionaries and explain them as a rational response to the shared and distinctive situation which confronts all revolutionaries.

Specifically, their minimal discussion of the motivations of the revolutionary implies that they view his motivations to be those universally shared by political leaders (and hence treat them as a constant)—personal and political survival, i.e., to stay alive and to stay in power. The situation confronted by the revolutionary is, however, viewed as distinctive because of the collapse of the two basic controls which limit conflict in stable societies—moral consensus and centralized coercion—and the resulting state of general anarchy and of open warfare among organized groups. The extreme behavior which we have called militance is then viewed as nothing more than the behavior necessary to recreate political order and hence ensure personal and political survival under these extreme conditions. The revolutionary is more dogmatic and populistic than the nonrevolutionary because he must formulate a new moral consensus and indoctrinate the masses in its tenets, under conditions of bitter ideological conflict. He is more cynical and elitist because he must recreate a system of centralized coercion, under conditions of anarchy and open warfare.[13]

This explanation is useful not only because it explains shared behavior in terms of a shared cause but also because of its ability to explain militance during the early stages of the revolution when the level of militance is low enough, and the level of political conflict is high enough, that militance does appear to be an appropriate response to the objective situation confronting the revolutionary. Its usefulness is limited, however, by its inability to explain the sharp increase in militance at precisely the point when the elimination of organized opposition and the restoration of order would seem to have reduced the situational necessity for such behavior.[14]

It is this increasing disparity in the later stages of the revolution between the necessities imposed by the objective situation and the behavior of the revolutionary which has induced some analysts to examine, in addition to the objective situation, the motivations which the revolutionary brings to that situation, and to reject the assumption that those motivations are limited to the minimal and universal ones of personal and political survival.

FAMILIAR MOTIVATIONS

The analysts who explain revolutionary behavior in terms of familiar motivations are persuaded that the motivations of the revolutionary do go beyond the minimal and universal motivations of personal and political survival and hence that those motivations must be examined explicitly. But they see the roots of revolutionary behavior in political motivations which, though accentuated, are still familiar enough that they do not feel the need to inquire into the antecedent causes of those motivations themselves. Specifically, they explain militant behavior by focusing on one of the elements of militance as the central motivation of the revolutionary and explaining the other elements of militance as being only the means for fully gratifying that central motivation.

Thus many of the students of totalitarianism (and many revolutionaries themselves) focus on ideological dogmatism and view the central motivation of the revolutionary as the drive to transform reality in the image of the ideology. The revolutionary is then viewed as being more populistic than the nonrevolutionary because of his drive to indoctrinate the masses in the ideology, and more cynical and elitist, i.e., more power-hungry, because of his willingness to use any short-term means to transform reality in the image of the ideology.[15]

Similarly, many of the students of mass society focus on populism and view the central motivation of the revolutionary as the drive for enthusiastic and unanimous mass support. The revolutionary is then viewed as being more dogmatic than the nonrevolutionary because he is catering to the alleged mass preference for simple explanations and for black and white moral distinctions, and more cynical and elitist, i.e., power-hungry, because he is catering to the alleged mass distaste for opposition and delay and to its admiration for strength and success.[16]

Finally, some of the other students of totalitarianism focus on cynicism and elitism and view the central motivation of the revolutionary as the drive for absolute power. The revolutionary is then viewed as being more dogmatic than the nonrevolutionary because of his drive to control minds as well as behavior, and more populistic because of his drive to monopolize control not only over the behavior and thoughts of the masses but also over every last ounce of their energy.[17]

This type of explanation is useful because it can explain more handily than can the theory of situational necessity the increase in militance after the elimination of organized opposition and the restoration of order seem to have reduced the necessity for it. For it views the revolutionary as a man with strong motivations in addition to the purely defensive ones of personal and political survival, who might very well view the removal of the major situational threats not as the occasion for quiescence but as the removal of the last obstacles to the full gratification of those motivations.

Its usefulness is limited, however, because the attempt to explain all of the extreme and conflicting behavior patterns that comprise militance in terms of a single motivation requires the analyst to balloon the motivation selected into something so extreme and so unusual (i.e., into something so *un*familiar) that that motivation then requires its own explantation. That is to say that ideological dogmatism which involves not only a willingness to derive all actions from the ideology and to indoctrinate and mobilize the entire populace in its behalf, but also a willingness to use any means to transform reality in its image, including those which directly conflict with the laws and utopia of the ideology itself, is a motivation which is unusual enough to require its own explanation. A populism which involves not only a willingness to glorify and identify with the masses but also a willingness to structure public policy in the image of the alleged simple-mindedness and power-lust of the masses, is a motivation unusual enough to require its own explanation. A drive for power which includes not only a pursuit of comprehensive and centralized control over the entire behavior of a people and complete unscrupulousness in the pursuit of that control, but also includes the attempt to completely control their minds and monopolize their energies, is a motivation which is unusual enough to require an explanation of its own.

It is precisely because these motivations seem so much more extreme in the revolutionary than do their counterparts in nonrevolutionaries that a number of analysts have attempted to follow the chain of causality back one more link, to ask about the causes of the motivations themselves.[18]

With this step they have, of course, moved into the realm of psychological theory. The two major types of psychological theories might be called, accurately if inelegantly, the theories of "cultural rejection-psychological void" and "childhood trauma-psychological conflict."

CULTURAL REJECTION–PSYCHOLOGICAL VOID

One of the two groups of psychopathologists who describe the revolutionary as mad man—the students of collective behavior—usually explains his behavior as the product of cultural rejection and a resultant state of psychological void.

This theory seems to be based on the assumption that men are born with few strong predispositions and that their adult behavior is gradually shaped by a learned "culture" composed of the two elements already noted in the descriptive section on psychopathology—"beliefs," or conceptions of what the world is like, which the individual uses to understand and manipulate his environment and which are accordingly necessary to his sense of effectiveness or power, and "values," or conceptions of how men ought to behave, which are necessary to his sense of worth or morality. Moreover, these beliefs and values acquire their capacity to shape the individual's behavior, and to provide him with a sense of power and morality, both because they are internalized in the individual himself as a result of the learning process and because they are supported by other individuals in the society with whom he abstractly or personally identifies.

Given this basic conception of human psychology, the initial cause of revolutionary militance is then viewed as cultural rejection—the rejection of the beliefs and values of the prevailing culture. The resultant psychological state is one of void—a confusion which results from the loss of these guidelines for effective and moral behavior and attendant doubts about one's power and morality (i.e., about one's ability to act effectively and morally).

The patterns of behavior which we have called militance are then viewed as ways of filling the void and specifically as replacements for the rejected culture, constructed in such a way as to restore the feelings of power and morality that it had once provided. Thus the revolutionary's dogmatic identification with the highly simplified beliefs and values of the ideology is viewed as an exaggerated attempt to replace the beliefs and values of the rejected culture and the feelings of power and morality they once provided. Similarly the revolutionary's populistic glorification of and identification with the masses is viewed as an exaggerated attempt to replace the social support for his sense of power and morality, which had been provided before his act of rebellion by the recognition that his beliefs and values were shared by most of the members of the society. The ruthless pursuit of power (cynicism and elitism) receives less emphasis in this theory than dogmatism and populism, but is sometimes treated as an additional source of reassurance about power and morality. For if the revolutionary can bolster his weakened sense of power and morality by completely identifying with, and indeed subordinating himself to, a set of ideas or group of people deemed to possess irresistible power and untarnished morality, he can also accomplish the same end by asserting his power over, and asserting his moral superiority to, these outside the movement or subordinate to himself within it.[19]

In this causal chain from cultural rejection to psychological void to militant behavior, cultural rejection seems more useful as an initial cause than does psychological void as an intervening psychological state. The notion of cultural rejection as an initial cause is engaging because it is convenient. It accounts for the striking correlation in a wide variety of contexts, discussed in the descriptive section, between revolution on the one hand and the patterns of militant behavior on the other, by viewing the act of revolution itself (and more precisely the cultural rejection which our definition of revolution necessarily implies) as the cause of militant behavior. In the process, it absolves us of the necessity of dealing with the difficult question of why men revolt—by implying that while men revolt for a wide variety of reasons (e.g. personal failure, societal crisis, acculturation, and so forth), marked similarities are burned into the behavior of all of them by the shared experience of revolution itself.

On the other hand, the concept of a void as an intervening psychological state lacks plausibility because of its inability to explain the extreme and continuing nature of militant behavior. It simply seems unlikely that the sense of confusion and doubt implied by that concept would generate sufficient motivation to account for the complete identification with a highly simplified set of beliefs and values and with a highly idealized conception of the masses, and the methodical and unscrupulous pursuit of comprehensive and centralized power, which together comprise militance. And even if it could account for such extreme behavior during the initial period of panic over the loss of behavioral guidelines, it clearly cannot account for the sharp increase in militance, discussed in the descriptive section, during the later stages of the revolution when the void would presumably have been filled by the elaboration of an ideology, the mobilization of some mass support, and the rise of the movement to power.[20]

The remaining psychological theory exhibits precisely the opposite pattern of strength and weakness, and hence raises the possibility of some combination of the two theories.

CHILDHOOD TRAUMA–PSYCHOLOGICAL CONFLICT

The other group of psychopathologists which describes the revolutionary as mad man—the students of individual neurosis—usually explain his behavior as the product of childhood trauma and a resultant state of psychological conflict.

In contrast to the basic conception of human psychology contained in the preceding theory, this theory is based on the Freudian assumption that men are born with a whole range of strong biological predispositions, many of which are socially unacceptable, and that those impulses, and hence adult behavior, are decisively shaped by controls imposed during early child-rearing before the age when culture is consciously learned. But in spite of these differences, the mechanisms which shape adult behavior in both theories are remarkably similar. The "ego," like "beliefs," comprises conceptions of what the world is like, which the individual uses to understand and manipulate his environment, and is accordingly necessary to his sense of effectiveness or power. The "superego," like "values," comprises conceptions of how men ought to behave and is necessary to the individual's sense of worth or morality. The ego and the superego, like beliefs and values, acquire their capacity to shape the individual's behavior, and to provide him with a sense of power and morality, both because they are introjected to become a part of the individual himself as a result of childhood training and because they are supported by his parents whom he loves and fears.

Given this basic conception of human psychology, the initial cause of revolutionary militance is then viewed as childhood trauma—the parental imposition of controls on biological impulses which are (1) harshly sanctioned, and (2) inadequately explained. The psychological state which results from the imposition of such controls is one of conflict—specifically the inordinate accentuation of the universal human conflict between socially unacceptable impulses and the controls on their expression. The fact that the controls are harshly sanctioned expands the range and power of the impulses which must be controlled by making the child so fearful that he suppresses an unusually broad range of biological impulses and by adding to those biological impulses a resentment against his parents which must also be fearfully repressed. The fact that the controls are inadequately explained weakens the child's ability to accept them as his own and hence to use them as controls on the now expanded set of unacceptable impulses.

There are two potentially revolutionary reactions to this state of abnormally sharp psychological conflict. The first is to cling fanatically to the ego and superego learned in childhood, as a means of repressing the unacceptable impulses which threaten them and, if this reaction is carried far enough, to become a revolutionary committeed to remaking society in the image of those purified traditional standards from which it has allegedly diverged. The other is to permit the open expression of the unacceptable impulses, and in particular of the rebellion against parental authority, to repress instead the ego and superego learned in childhood, and if this reaction is carried far enough, to become a revolutionary committed to remaking society in the image of a new set of standards. In either case, the revolutionary will continue to suffer from a psychological conflict between the standards for effective and moral behavior contained in his current ego and superego (whether those be the ones learned in childhood or new ones constructed after rebellion) and unacceptable impulses which threaten those standards (whether those be biological impulses and resentment against parents or the now rejected and repressed ego and superego learned in childhood), and from attendant doubts about power and morality which are in some respects similar to those postulated by the notion of psychological void. The difference is that the doubts about power and morality implied by the concept of psychological conflict are more powerful than those implied by the concept of psychological void—because they result not only from a weakening of the guidelines for effective and moral behavior but from that plus an assault on those guidelines by powerful impulses which threaten to drive the revolutionary into what he views as dangerous and immoral behavior.

As a result, the patterns of behavior which we have called militance are viewed not only as replacements for the weakened or rejected ego and superego, constructed in such a way as to create the feelings of power and morality that they had never provided, but also as controls, constructed in such a way as to keep unacceptable impulses and the doubts about power and morality they engender out of the conscious mind.

Dogmatism and populism receive less emphasis in this theory than in the theory of psychological void, but to the degree that they are treated, they are explained in essentially the same way as in that theory (in spite of differences in terminology)—as exaggerated replacement respectively for the old ego-superego standards of effective and moral behavior and for the social support (in this case parental support) which those standards enjoyed.

Cynicism and elitism receive much more emphasis than in the previous theory and are viewed as controls on the revolutionary's own doubts about power and morality and on relationships with those elements of society which might arouse those doubts. Hence the refusal to accept even the power and moral limitations on his behavior which are implied by his own ideology, which we have called cynicism, is viewed as the revolutionary's attempt to control potentially paralyzing doubts about power and morality which even the slightest concession might release. The pursuit of comprehensive power over society, its centralization in a few hands, and its use for a terrorist assault on those outside the circle of trust, which we have called elitism, is viewed as the revolutionary's attempt to control his relationships with those elements of society which might arouse potentially paralyzing impulses and doubts:

(1) by dividing the world into ingroup and outgroup and permitting no compromise between the two—to avoid contaminating contact,

(2) by insisting on the absolute goodness of the ingroup and on the absolute submission of the individual to it—to bolster his own weak controls over impulses with external organizational controls, and

(3) by seeing his own unacceptable impulses and doubts, not as part of himself, but as a part of those objects or people who arouse those feelings in him—to project those impulses and doubts which he cannot control away from himself. [21]

In this causal chain from childhood trauma to psychological conflict to militant behavior, psychological conflict seems more useful as an intervening psychological state than does childhood trauma as an initial cause. Specifically, the general concept of psychological conflict between guidelines for effective and moral behavior and impulses which threaten to produce dangerous and immoral behavior (without raising the question of the validity of Freudian ideas about the specific origins and content of that conflict), seems better able to account for the extreme and continuing nature of militant behavior than does the concept of void.

It provides a more plausible explanation for the extreme nature of militant behavior because, as we have already noted, such a conflict implies more powerful doubts and hence more extreme measures to deal with them. Similarly, and more important, it provides a more plausible explanation for the continuing and intensifying pattern of militance. For while it seems implausible that a man whose militance derived from a void would continue and intensify militant behavior after that void has been filled by the elaboration of an ideology, the attraction of mass support, and the consolidation of power, such behavior seems more plausible on the part of a man whose militance derives from a conflict with impulses and doubts which are an ineradicable part of himself and from a conflict which accordingly may sharpen as he uses his increasing power to extend his attack on the remnants of the old order in society and in himself.[22]

On the other hand (even if the difficulty of finding adequate data on the childhood of revolutionaries is ignored), childhood trauma as an initial cause seems less useful than does cultural rejection. Whereas the concept of cultural rejection accounts for the clear covariation, noted in the descriptive section, between revolution on the one hand and militant behavior on the other, by the simple device of viewing the former as the cause of the latter, the concept of childhood trauma has difficulty accounting for that covariation, or indeed for any variation in the amount of militant behavior over time. For, barring radical shifts in child-rearing practices, it implies the production of a pool of revolutionary militants which will be relatively constant in size whatever the social conditions and attendant adult experiences. This difficulty could, of course, be overcome by arguing that childhood trauma does indeed produce a relatively constant pool of individuals with propensities for militant behavior, and that the apparent variations in amounts of militant behavior at the societal level result from the fact that such individuals become visible only at times of revolutionary turmoil when those propensities are triggered into successful political action. But once it is conceded that the revolutionary experience itself can trigger militant behavior in some individuals who previously had only a propensity in that direction, the possibility is clearly raised that the revolutionary experience can also create militant behavior in many individuals with no previously discernible propensity for such behavior—which is, of course, precisely what the concept of cultural rejection implies.[23]

Thus while cultural rejection seems more plausible as an initial cause than does childhood trauma, psychological conflict seems more plausible as an intervening psychological state than does psychological void. The synthetic theory proposed here will accordingly attempt to explain revolutionary militance as the product of cultural rejection and a resultant state of psychological conflict.

A SYNTHETIC EXPLANATION

Our review of the explanations for revolutionary militance has moved from a focus on unique causal factors to a focus on two types of shared causal factors—the external situation confronting the revolutionary and the motivations which the revolutionary brings to that situation. Our review of the theory of situational necessity suggested that the situation confronting the revolutionary differs from that confronting the nonrevolutionary because of the breakdown in centralized coercion and in moral consensus and the unlimited conflict over power and morality which results. Our review of the various motivational theories now seems to suggest that the motivations of the revolutionary differ from those of the nonrevolutionary because the unlimited conflict over power and morality characteristic of the revolutionary's external situation is echoed by a similar conflict within the revolutionary himself.

A theory of cultural rejection—psychological conflict can be used to explain why this is so. Both the students of collective behavior and the students of individual neurosis agree, in spite of differences in terminology, that all reasonably stable societies are supported by a culture, i.e., by a widely shared set of beliefs and values which regulate the behavior of the individuals who comprise the society and provide them with a sense of power and morality. They also agree that these beliefs and values have a hold on the individual because they are internalized and become a part of himself and because they are supported by a large number of other individuals with whom he abstractly or personally identifies, and hence become a part of the society which he confronts.

The act of revolution, therefore, necessarily brings the revolutionary into conflict with those aspects of *himself* and of his *society* which are still tied to the old beliefs and values. That is to say that the act of revolution usually requires the revolutionary to reject most of what he has been taught since childhood and to reject, attack, and often kill those who taught it to him and those who continue to believe it. Because this usually involves attacks not only on the hated and distant elite but also on family, friends, the masses in whose name the revolution has been made, and sometimes even members of his own revolutionary movement, the act of revolution necessarily generates a good deal of anguish and doubt. More specifically, in his confrontation with both his old self and with others still tied to the old society, the revolutionary's attacks on the old beliefs (guidelines for effective behavior) produce doubts about the movement's *power* to succeed, while attacks on the old values (guidelines for moral behavior) produce doubts about the *morality* of doing so. In short, revolution necessarily involves the revolutionary in a conflict between his rejection of the old culture and its continuing hold on him and his society and hence generates potentially paralyzing doubts about power and morality. At the same time it creates an unlimited external conflict over power and morality in the midst of which the revolutionary cannot afford such doubts and the hesitation they might induce.

It is this combination of internal doubts and an external situation in which they are intolerable which imposes on the revolutionary a distinctive central motivation—an attempt to overcome those doubts in his movement and in himself by a pursuit of power and morality more extreme than that of nonrevolutionaries. The distinctive behavior patterns (i.e., the elements of militance) which result from this distinctive motivation revolve, as the previous two psychological theories have indicated, around the dual tasks of constructing a *replacement* for the old culture and imposing rigid *controls* on doubts until the old culture can be destroyed and the revolutionary replacement established in its stead.

Ideology is the revolutionary's replacement for the internalized culture, rendered dogmatic by his exaggerated need to reassure his followers and himself about the power and morality of the movement. Hence,

(1) he replaces the beliefs of the old culture with deterministic laws which guarantee victory—in order to provide reassurance about the power of the movement to succeed,

(2) he replaces the values of the old culture with a morally perfect utopia in behalf of which any action is justified—in order to provide reassurance about the morality of the movement's actions, and

(3) he logically derives all actions from the ideology and claims infallibility in that interpretive process—in order to identify the movement with the irresistible power and unquestionable morality of the ideology's laws and utopia.

Similarly, *populism* is the revolutionary's replacement for the social support which derived in the old society from the recognition that his beliefs and values were shared by most of that society—rendered extreme, once again, by his exaggerated need to reassure his followers and himself about the power and morality of the movement. Hence,

(1) he views the emancipated masses as the key to unlimited power—in order to provide reassurance about the power of the movement to succeed,

(2) he views the emancipated masses as the key ultimate morality—in order to provide reassurance about the morality of the movement's actions, and

(3) he logically rejects any distinction between the movement and the masses and organizes active mass participation and periodic demonstrations of mass support—in order to identify the movement with the irresistible power and untarnished morality of the masses.

But the construction of these replacements for the old culture and its social support cannot break the hold of the old order alone. Because of the tenacity of that hold on both the revolutionaries themselves and on the society they confront, and the potentially paralyzing doubts generated by that hold, the revolutionary must also impose a set of controls on those doubts until the old culture can be destroyed and the revolutionary replacement established in its stead.

Cynicism results from the revolutionary's need to control the doubts of the revolutionaries themselves. Hence,

(1) he rejects all power limitations on the actions of the movement, including those implied by the laws of his own ideology, in favor of an extreme voluntarism which asserts the omnipotence of revolutionary fervor—in order to control doubts about power which might lead to outright capitulation before the power of the old order or (more often) to an indefinite postponement of revolutionary action until the laws of history have progressed to the point of assuring easy success;

(2) he rejects all moral limitations on the actions of the movement, including those implied by the utopia of his own ideology, in favor of an amoral instrumentalism which measures morality solely in terms of contribution to the power of the movement—in order to control doubts about morality which might lead to outright capitulation before the moral authority of the old culture or (more often) to a paralyzing refusal to violate the purified standards of morality contained in the utopia.

Elitism results from the revolutionary's need to control the relationship of the movement with the old society, and in particular from the need to protect the movement from being seduced and smothered by the enormous physical and moral force emanating from the continuing hold of the old culture on the bulk of that society. Hence,

(1) he rejects all power compromise in favor of a demand for comprehensive control, not only over organized political groups (the active power of the old order) but also over the daily lives of the masses (the passive power of the old order)—in order to control the temptation to accept an inevitably unequal compromise with the power of the old order;

(2) he similarly rejects all moral compromise in favor of the centralization of control in the hands of those very few individuals sufficiently immune to the moral authority of the old culture to be trustworthy—in order to control the temptation to capitulate to the morality of the old culture (a temptation heightened by the immersion of the movement in the old society in the pursuit of comprehensive control).

Specifically, the revolutionary attempts to protect the movement from moral compromise with the old society in which it is immersed in three ways—all of which contribute to centralized control:

(a) He insists on a rigid mental and organizational demarcation between the movement and the outside world, denies the possibility of any middle ground, and thus excludes from the circle of trust and power both the passive masses (viewed as carriers of the old culture) and active sympathizers who will not submit to the absolute discipline of the movement (viewed as bridges back to the old culture)—in order to avoid any fuzzing of the conflict between the movement and the old society which might pave the way for the seduction of the former by the latter.

(b) Within the movement, he insists on absolute obedience to the leadership and exludes from the circle of trust and power anyone who openly opposes that leadership as well as those faithful but weary veterans who, as the cutting edge of the movement, have been buried in contaminated society so long that their continued reliability is open to question—in order to bolster the weak will of the individual operative against the allure of the old morality by encasing him in an iron sheath of organizational discipline.

(c) The third device used to protect the movement against moral compromise occurs only at the peak of militance and largely because of the centralization of control, and responsibility, resulting from the first two. For the insistence on absolute obedience to the center forces the leader to assume personal moral responsibility for all the actions of the movement, i.e., to take upon himself the doubts about morality of the entire movement, and at the same time makes the movement so dependent upon the leader that he must divest himself of all doubts lest his hesitation paralyze the entire movement. As a result of this combination of growing doubts and growing inability to tolerate them, the revolutionary comes to project his own doubts about morality (i.e., his feelings of guilt) onto those outside the circle of trust and power who arouse those feelings in him. He then directs against them a violence that is terroristic in the sense that it is noncalcuable (because targets are selected on the basis of the feelings of guilt they arouse in the revolutionary and not on the basis of their actions), continuous (because the image of the enemy results from the projection of the revolutionary's own sense of guilt and hence grows rather than diminishes with the extermination of each new set of enemies), and brutal (because the enemy is endowed with precisely those characteristics so hated that the revolutionary cannot even tolerate the suspicion that they might be a part of himself).

This explanation of the distinctive patterns of revolutionary behavior in terms of cultural rejection and a resultant state of psychological conflict, is summarized in Figure 2.

Just as it is possible to make sense of the static pattern of militant behavior so consistently affirmed in the descriptive literature in terms of the psychological and situational conflict caused by revolution, so too is it possible to make sense of the rise and decline in the level of that militance, also noted in the descriptive literature, in terms of a rise and decline in the sharpness of that conflict.

Thus we might speculate that the relatively low level of militance which is apparently characteristic of the initial period after the collapse of the old regime, in spite of the anarchy and open warfare which is sometimes characteristic of the objective situation confronting the revolutionary during this stage, reflects the fact that the initial leadership among the discontented elements of a society usually falls to those whose respected positions within the existing society give them greater initial political effectiveness. But that position also spares them much of the psychological conflict usually associated with the act of revolution—either because it induces them to limit their rejection of the old society or, if that rejection remains comprehensive, because they are frequently members of an alienated but respected subculture (e.g., the Westernized intellectuals in Russia and in the former colonial areas or the military in Germany) and hence are protected from a confrontation with the hold of the old culture on themselves and on the society, by socialization since childhood in the alienated subculture and by the cordon of like-thinking individuals who constitute the subculture and isolate them from the rest of the society.

We might then interpret the regular displacement of this group by individuals who exhibit the full range of militant characteristics to be not only the result of the deteriorating objective situation but also the result of the fact that most individuals do not live within the safe harbor of an alienated subculture. For most individuals the act of revolution does generate the conflict with the old self and the old society which we have described. Thus as more and more individuals reject the old culture, the sheer weight of numbers may shift the control of the movement toward those for whom revolution does involve this psychological conflict and the militant behavior which results from it.

The idea that militant behavior is grounded as much in psychological as in situational conflict can even shed light on the third and most mystifying of the stages noted in the descriptive literature—the sharp increase in militance at precisely the point at which the elimination of organized opposition and the restoration of order would seem to have eliminated the situational necessity for it. For it is precisely at this point, when the

REPLACEMENT
For Old Self-Ideological Dogmatism

(1) Deterministic laws

(2) Utopia

(3) Complete identification with
  ideology
  —Logically
  —Factually

CONTROL
Over Old Self-Cynicism

(1) Voluntarism

(2) Instrumentalism
  —Counterutopia

For Old Society-Populism

(1) Emancipated masses as key to
  unlimited power

(2) Emancipated masses as key to
  ultimate morality

Over Relations with Old Society-Elitism

(1) Comprehensive control[
  —Over organized opposition
  —Over daily lives of masses

(2) Centralized control
  —Exclusion of passive masses
  —Exclusion of active sympa-
    thizer
  —Exclusion within the move-
    ment
    —of opponents
    —of the faithful but
      weary
    —of all but the leader
  —Terror against the excluded
    —noncalculable violence
    —continuous violence
    —brutal violence

(3) Complete identification with
  masses
  —Logically
  —Factually

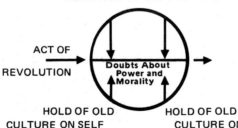

REJECTION OF OLD CULTURE

ACT OF
REVOLUTION

Doubts About
Power and
Morality

HOLD OF OLD
CULTURE ON SELF

HOLD OF OLD
CULTURE ON SOCIETY

Figure 2

conflict with organized opposition is eliminated, that the psychological conflict of the revolutionary may begin its sharpest rise. If the previous assumption about the nature and tenacity of the old culture's hold is correct, then the elimination of organized opposition will make it fully clear for the first time that the hold of the old culture on the mass of the people in the society has not been broken by the construction of replacements for it and by the destruction of those groups which had enforced it, and that the revolutionaries must now either abandon many of the goals of the revolution or launch an attack on the masses themselves and on those in the movement who balk at that prospect. If the decision is made to push ahead with the remaking of the masses, then the combination of the revolutionary's expanded awareness of the old culture's hold on the masses together with his expanded attacks on them may very well increase the level of psychological conflict, the level of doubts about the power of the movement to succeed and about the morality of its actions, and the resultant level of militant behavior, even though organized opposition and disorder have been eliminated.

Just as the concept of psychological conflict can help to make sense of the apparent divergence, with which this third stage begins, between the revolutionary's behavior and the demands of the objective situation, so too can it help to make sense of the growth of that divergence by the end of this stage to a point which has led some analysts to view such men as Hitler, Stalin, and Robespierre as insane. For as the revolutionary expands the definition of the enemy and the targets of his attacks beyond his organized opposition to include the masses in whose name he has always fought and some of the revolutionary brothers who have fought by his side, his doubts about his power to succeed and about the morality of his actions may very well rise to the point where his behavior is more and more dominated by his personal psychological needs and less and less by the demands of the objective situation he confronts. An additional indication of this is the fact that most of the characteristics usually used to support the charge of insanity might also be viewed simply as extensions of the characteristics of militance to the point where they snap the revolutionary's grasp of reality. Thus the raising of the ideology above discussion to the level of a sacrosanct doctrine might be viewed as an extension of dogmatism; the insistence on mass adulation of the leader's person, as an extension of populism; omnipotence fantasies and the refusal to hear unpleasant facts, as an extension of the rejection of all power and moral limitations on revolutionary action, which we have called cynicism; and megalomania and terror, as an extension of the drive for comprehensive and centralized power, which we have called elitism. This explanation permits us to discard the view of the revolutionary at the peak of militance as a lunatic who inexplicably rose to a position of absolute power and to view him more plausibly as a man burned out by his own revolutionary efforts, as the last victim of his own revolution.

Finally, the idea that militant behavior is rooted in a conflict between the revolutionary's rejection of the old culture and its continuing hold on him and on his society can also help to make sense of the last stage of the revolution—the apparent inability of the original generation of revolutionary leaders to use their complete control over the socialization processes to instill militance in their successors and the resultant decline of militance after this generation of leaders who made the revolution has been displaced. For to the degree that the movement's socialization of the younger generation is successful, it will weaken and eventually eliminate the hold of the old culture on the inheritors themselves and on the society they confront, and with it, the militance which grows out of the struggle against that hold. When, at the end of this stage of declining militance, power passes to individuals born after the revolution and socialized since childhood in its ideology, militant behavior should therefore shade back into nonrevolutionary patterns of political behavior, albeit within the context of a reconstituted culture.

The rise of these children of the revolution to leadership will therefore be both a triumph and a defeat for the fathers of the revolution. A triumph in the sense that this generation will have internalized most of the content of the revolutionary ideology and, in this sense, will represent the completion of the revolutionary task of remaking man. A defeat, in the sense that the fiery old revolutionaries, who struggled to mold the younger generation in their likeness, will bring forth a generation lacking in the central element of that likeness—the fire.

NOTES

1. The meaning of this definition of revolution will be spelled out in greater detail when the concepts of "culture" and "cultural rejection" are introduced later in the paper, but it is roughly synonymous with the most fundamental type of revolution as defined by a number of students of the subject. See the concepts of "great revolutions" in Pettee (1938: 1-29); "rebellion" in Merton (1957: 131-160); "structural war" in Rosenau (1964: 60-63); "total revolution" in Johnson (1966: 135-149).

2. The clearest examples of this description in the literature on collective behavior are Smelser (1963); Cantril (1963). See also Toch (1965). It should be

noted that there are students of collective behavior who implicitly or explicitly reject the idea that collective behavior is pathological or even different in appearance than behavior within accepted social norms. See Blumer (1951); Turner (1964); Couch (1968). The clearest example of this description in the literature that compares the revolutionary to the individual neurotic is Adorno et al. (1950: 1-270). See also Christie and Cook (1958); Wolfenstein (1967). There are additional significant works in both these groups, but inasmuch as they focus more on explanation than description, they will be noted in the section on explanation.

3. For an argument that Fascist and Communist revolutionaries are the penultimate representatives of the twentieth-century tendency to believe in the omnipotence and virtue of the masses, see Ortega y Gasset (1932). For an argument that the early stages of both Fascist and Communist movements are characterized by an extreme mutual dependence of the leadership and the mass following, see Kornhauser (1959). For an argument that the Fascists pursued enthusiastic and unanimous mass support as their central goal, see Lederer (1940).

4. The major recent works on totalitarianism are Arendt (1966); Friedrich and Brzezinski (1966); Friedrich (1954); Buchheim (1968). These works build on the earlier works, Cobban (1939); Neumann (1965). Works which attempt to find historical counterparts to totalitarianism are Talmon (1960a, 1960b); Cohn (1961); Wittfogel (1957); Moore (1958).

5. For the deterministic laws of the ideology, see the concepts of "ideology" in Arendt (1966: 460-479); "myth" and "action-oriented programs" in Friedrich and Brzezinski (1966: 85-97); Buchheim (1968: 11-37). For the importance of utopias to revolutionary ideologies and a description of their typical content, see esp. Cohn (1961); Talmon (1960b). See also the concept of "utopia" in Friedrich and Brzezinski (1966: 22, 85-97); Buchheim (1968:56-73). For identification with the ideology by logically deriving all actions from it, see the concept of the drive for "consistency" in Arendt (1966: 460-479). For identification with the ideology by altering reality to protect the infallibility of one's ideological interpretations, see esp. the concept of the "fictitious world" in Arendt (1966: 241-459). See also the concept of "unpolitical thinking" in Buchheim (1968: 74-88); Friedrich and Brzezinski (1966: 98-106).

6. For the similarities between democracy and totalitarianism, see Cobban (1939); Neumann (1965: esp. 1-9); the concept of "mass legitimation" in Friedrich and Brzezinski (1966: 3-14); Eckstein and Apter (1963). For logical identification with the masses, see Talmon (1960b); and the concept of "popular sovereignty" in Cobban (1939: esp. 50-109). For identification with the masses by making enthusiastic and unanimous support a visible fact, see the concept of the "passion for unanimity" in Friedrich and Brzezinski (1966: 161-171); Talmon (1960b); Arendt (1966: 305-341, 474-479).

7. For the substitution of voluntarism for the laws of the ideology, see the muted suspicions to this effect in Friedrich and Brzezinski (1966: 107-115); and the explicit charge of "cynicism" based on the belief that "all is possible" in Arendt (1966: 364-388). For the substitution of instrumentalism for the utopia of the ideology, see the argument that revolutionary goals are inevitably perverted in Buchheim (1968: 103-109); the argument that it is a commitment to the struggle itself that displaces those goals in Neumann (1965), Cassinelli (1960); and the argument that "all is permitted" in the interests of the organization necessary to win that struggle in Arendt (1966: 364-388, 460-479).

8. On comprehensive control. For the refusal to tolerate any organized opposition, domestic or international, and the way in which this distinguishes totalitarianism from traditional autocracy, see Neumann (1965: 137-141, 257-310); Talmon (1960b: 118-121, 129-131); Friedrich and Brzezinski (1966: 353-366); Arendt (1966: 415-418); Feierabend (1962). For the insistence on control over the daily lives of the masses—their thoughts as well as their behavior, see Neumann (1957); Cobban (1939: 161-188); Neumann (1965: 1-9); Friedrich and Brzezinski (1966: 15-27); Arendt (1966: 389-459); Buchheim (1968: 11-37); Talmon (1960b: 132-148).

On centralized control. For a general picture of the continuous exclusion of more and more of the society from the circle of trust and power, see the concept of the movement as "onion-like" in Arendt (1966: 364-388). For the exclusion of the masses, see the concepts of rule by the "functionaries" in Buchheim (1966: 103-109); "exclusivist" party in Friedrich and Brzezinski (1966: 45-59); and the argument that this occurs even in the most democratically oriented revolutions in Talmon (1960b: esp. 98-131). For the exclusion and surveillance of active sympathizers, see the descriptions of the device of multiple bureaucracies in Friedrich and Brzezinski (1966: 205-218); Buchheim (1968: 89-102); Talmon (1960b: 122-127). For the exclusion of those within the movement guilty of oppositional actions or suspected of oppositional thought, see Friedrich and Brzezinski (1966: 45-59, 183-202); Arendt (1966: 364-388); Buchheim (1968: 31-37); Talmon (1960b: 118-121, 127-129). For the resultant centralization power in the hands of one man, his emancipation from responsibility to higher principle, from responsibility to the masses, and from responsibility to the movement, see respectively Friedrich and Brzezinski (1966: 31-44); Cobban (1939: 27-50, 161-188); Neumann (1965: 42-54); Arendt (1966: 364-419). For the application of terroristic violence against targets who are neither actual nor potential oppositionists, see the concepts of "noncalculable" violence in Neumann (1957: 245); "enemies of the people" in Friedrich and Brzezinski (1966: 172-182); "objective enemies" and "random" victims in Arendt (1966: 389-459). For the continuous appearance of new targets for terroristic violence, see Friedrich and Brzezinski (1966: 172-182); Arendt (1966: 309-311, 437-459); Talmon (1960b: 80-83, 127-129). For the level of physical and psychological brutality involved in terroristic violence, see Arendt (1966: 437-439).

9. The most influential of the sociologies of revolution which grew out of the revolutionary aftermath of World War I are Brinton (1956); Pettee (1938); Edwards (1965); Sorokin (1925). More recent works are Johnson (1964, 1966); Leiden and Schmitt (1968).

10. The only conscious attempt to construct a coherent picture of the revolutionary at the peak of militance and the clearest confirmation of the pattern of militance already described is Brinton (1956: 154-214, esp. 162-168). See also Pettee (1938: 13-24, 127-139); Killian (1964); Wallace (1956: 148-152). For the stages of that militance, see the concepts of the "era of optimism," "reign of terror," and "return to normality" in Edwards (1965: 98-209); the "stateless period," "terror and dictatorship," and "thermidor" in Pettee (1938: 106-151); and "rule of the moderates," "reign of terror and virtue," and "thermidor" in Brinton (1956: 128-249).

11. For the assertion by the students of totalitarianism that militance, and in particular terror, is maintained and indeed increases when organized opposition has been eliminated and order restored, see the concepts of "permanent revolution" in Neumann (1965), and in Lowenthal (1960); "laws of movement" in Arendt (1960:

460-479); "totalitarian breakthrough" in Friedrich and Brzezinski (1961: 172-182, 293-303); Talmon (1960b: 132-138). The selective empirical focus of the sociologists of revolution has been noted in the text. For the tendency to construe the emergence of cynicism and elitism as the end of the revolution, see the discussion of the characteristics of thermidor in Brinton (1956: 215-250). For their difficulty in applying the prediction of an early decline in militance to Russia, see Brinton (1956: 215-250); Edwards (1965: 186-209); Pettee (1938: 141-151).

12. For the revision of the notions of perpetual militance in light of the post-Stalinist period, see the concept of "oscillation" in Friedrich and Brzezinski (1966: 161-171, 367-378); Arendt (1966: xviii-xxi).

13. The clearest examples of this kind of explanation are Pettee (1938: 13-24, 106-123, 127-139, 144-146); Edwards (1965: 90-97, 186-209); Amann (1962).

14. For evidence that militance does increase sharply at the point where the situational necessity for it declines sharply, and for the inability of the sociologists of revolution to deal with that fact either in terms of description or explanation, see the citations in n. 11.

15. For a focus on dogmatism generally as the central motivation see Buchheim (1968: 11-37, 103-109); Friedrich and Brzezinski (1966: 102-103, 105, 161-171). For a focus on the laws of the ideology, see Arendt (1966: 460-479); Inkeles (1954). For a focus on the utopia of the ideology, see Talmon (1960b: esp. 1-13).

16. For a focus on populism as the central motivation, see Lederer (1940: 153-157, 235-240, 23-46, 98-131); Mannheim (1940: 39-75, 117-143); and Ortega y Gasset (1932: 107-117, 137-204, 75-84).

17. For a focus on absolute power as the central motivation, see Neumann (1965: 230-256); Wittfogel (1957: 1-10); Moore (1958); Cassinelli (1960).

18. Even among those analysts who use familiar motivation explanations, there is frequently muted recognition that those motivations themselves require an explanation. With respect to dogmatism, see the open admission that they have not provided an explanation in Friedrich and Brzezinski (1966: vii-viii); and the move toward a psychological explanation in Arendt (1966: 305-340, 474-479). With respect to populism, see the explicit recognition of the need for a social-psychological explanation in Mannheim (1940: 39-75). With respect to power, see the massive and reluctant demonstrations that the familiar level of power drive does *not* produce all the elements of militance, even when completely unfettered, in Wittfogel (1957); Moore (1958); the movement toward a psychological explanation of that power drive in Neumann (1965: 230-256); and the explanatory contortions imposed by the refusal to move in that direction in Cassinelli (1960).

19. For the explanation of dogmatism in these terms, see Smelser (1963); Cantril (1963); Toch (1965: 28-44, 130-156); Walzer (1963: 61-88). For a similar explanation of dogmatism and populism, see Hoffer (1951). For a similar explanation of dogmatism but especially of populism and the pursuit of power, see Fromm (1941).

20. The inability of this explanation to account for the increase in militance after the void has been filled, is indicated by the fact that none of these works treat that rise in militance or indeed any aspect of the varying levels of militance, save for Hoffer (1951: 119-138), and he drops his psychological explanation in favor of a situational one on this issue.

21. For an explanation in these terms of dogmatism and populism on the one hand and cynicism and elitism on the other, but which sees them as characteristics of

two separate types of political men, see the concepts of the "agitator" and the "administrator" in Lasswell (1962: 7-58, 59-93, 148-173); Lasswell (1960: 78-152); Lasswell (1958: 131-147). For an explanation of the whole pattern of militance in these terms and an argument that all of the elements can exist in a single type of political man, see Adorno et al. (1950: 222-279, 337-389, 468-488). For similar explanations of militance but which focus on men who opt for radicalism rather than reaction, see Wolfenstein (1967); Bychowski (1948).

22. For the continuation and intensification of militance as a result of the ineradicable nature of the conflict, see Wolfenstein (1967: 240-301); and Bychowski (1940: 35-116, 212-241).

23. For concessions from analysts who focus on childhood trauma that social crisis and attendant adult experiences may be necessary to trigger militant behavior in individuals with a propensity for it, see Adorno et al. (1950: 4-5, 972); Lasswell (1962: 174-205); Wolfenstein (1967: 16, 22-23, 101-102); Bychowski (1948: 242-252). For concessions from the same type of analysts that social crises and attendant adult experiences might be capable of creating militance in individuals with no such propensity, see Strole (1951); Lasswell (1962: 39-44, 161-168); Gilbert (1950: 3-15).

REFERENCES

ADORNO, T. W., E. FRENKEL-BRUNSWICK, D. J. LEVINSON, and R. N. SANFORD (1950) The Authoritarian Personality. New York: Harper & Bros.

AMANN, P. (1962) "Revolution: a redefinition." Pol. Sci. Q. 77 (March): 36-53.

ARENDT, H. (1966) The Origins of Totalitarianism. New York: Harcourt, Brace & World.

BLUMER, H. (1951) "Collective behavior," pp. 167-222 in A.M. Lee (ed.) The Principles of Sociology. New York: Barnes & Noble.

BRINTON, C. (1956) Anatomy of Revolution. New York: Random House.

BUCHHEIM, H. (1968) Totalitarian Rule (R. Hein, trans.). Middletown, Conn.: Wesleyan Univ. Press.

BYCHOWSKI, G. (1948) Dictators and Disciples. New York: International Universities Press.

CANTRIL, H. (1963) The Psychology of Social Movements. New York: John Wiley.

CASSINELLI, C. W. (1960) "Totalitarianism, ideology and propaganda." J. of Politics 22 (February): 68-95.

CHRISTIE, R. and P. COOK (1958) "A guide to the published literature relating to the authoritarian personality through 1956." J. of Psychology 45-46: 171-201.

COBBAN, A. (1939) Dictatorship. New York: Charles Scribner's Sons.

COHN, N. (1961) The Pursuit of the Millenium. New York: Harper & Bros.

COUCH, C. J. (1968) "Collective behavior: an examination of some stereotypes." Social Problems 15 (Winter): 310-322.

ECKSTEIN, H. and D. E. APTER (1963) "Totalitarianism and autocracy: introduction," pp. 433-440 in H. Eckstein and D. E. Apter (eds.) Comparative Politics. New York: Free Press.

EDWARDS, L. P. (1965) The Natural History of Revolution. New York: Russell & Russell.

FEIERABEND, I. K. (1962) "Expansionistic and isolationistic tendencies in totalitarianism." J. of Politics 24 (November): 733-742.

FRIEDRICH, C. J. [ed.] (1954) Totalitarianism. Cambridge: Harvard Univ. Press.

––– and Z. K. BRZEZINSKI (1966) Totalitarian Dictatorship and Autocracy. New York: Frederick A. Praeger.

––– (1961) Totalitarian Dictatorship and Autocracy. New York: Frederick A. Praeger.

FROMM, E. (1941) Escape From Freedom. New York: Rinehart.

GILBERT, G. M. (1950) The Psychology of Dictatorship. New York: Roland Press.

HOFFER, E. (1951) The True Believer. New York: Harper & Bros.

INKELES, A. (1954) "The totalitarian mystique," pp. 87-108 in C. J. Friedrich (ed.) Totalitarianism. Cambridge: Harvard Univ. Press.

JOHNSON, C. (1966) Revolutionary Change. Boston: Little, Brown.

––– (1964) Revolution and the Social System. Stanford: Hoover Institution.

KILLIAN, L. M., (1964) "Social movements," pp. 426-455 in R. E. Farris (ed.) Handbook of Modern Sociology. Chicago: Rand McNally.

KORNHAUSER, W. (1959) The Politics of Mass Society. New York: Free Press.

LASSWELL, H. (1962) Power and Personality. New York: Viking Press.

––– (1960) Psychopathology and Politics. New York: Viking Press.

––– (1958) Politics. Cleveland: World.

LEDERER, E. (1940) State of the Masses. New York: W. W. Norton.

LEIDEN, C. and K. SCHMITT (1968) The Politics of Violence. Englewood Cliffs, N.J.: Prentice-Hall.

LOWENTHAL, R. (1960) "Totalitarianism reconsidered." Commentary 29: 504-512.

MANNHEIM, K. (1940) Man and Society in the Age of Reconstruction. New York: Harcourt, Brace.

MERTON, R. (1957) Social Theory and Social Structure. New York: Free Press.

MOORE, B., Jr. (1958) "Totalitarian elements in pre-industrial societies," pp. 30-88 in B. Moore, Jr. (ed.) Political Power and Social Theory. Cambridge: Harvard Univ. Press.

NEUMANN, S. (1965) Permanent Revolution. New York: Frederick A. Praeger.

NEUMANN, F. (1957) "Notes on the theory of dictatorship," pp. 233-256 in F. Neumann (ed.) The Democratic and the Authoritarian State. New York: Free Press.

ORTEGA y GASSET, J. (1932) The Revolt of the Masses. New York: W. W. Norton.

PETTEE, G. S. (1938) The Process of Revolution. New York: Harper & Bros.

ROSENAU, J. [ed.] (1964) International Aspects of Civil Strife. Princeton: Princeton Univ. Press.

SMELSER, N. (1963) Theory of Collective Behavior. New York: Free Press.

SOROKIN, P. A. (1925) The Sociology of Revolution. Philadephia: J. P. Lippincott.

STROLE, L. (1951) "Social dysfunction, personality, and social distance attitudes." Paper presented at the convention of the American Sociological Society. (unpublished)

TALMON, J. L. (1960a) Political Messianism. New York: Frederick A. Praeger.

––– (1960b) The Origins of Totalitarian Democracy. New York: Frederick A. Praeger.

TOCH, H. (1965) The Social Psychology of Social Movements. Indianapolis: Bobbs-Merrill.

TURNER, R. (1964) "Collective behavior," pp. 382-425 in R. E. Farris (ed.) Handbook of Modern Sociology. Chicago: Rand McNally.

WALLACE, A. F. C. (1956) "Revitalization movements." American Anthropologist 58 (April): 264-281.

WALZER, M. (1963) "Puritanism as a revolutionary ideology." History & Theory 3 (1): 61-88.

WITTFOGEL, K. A. (1957) Oriental Despotism. New Haven: Yale Univ. Press.

WOLFENSTEIN, E. V. (1967) The Revolutionary Personality. Princeton: Princeton Univ. Press.

WILLIAM T. DALY is assistant professor and coordinator of the political science program at Stockton State College. He has received a series of awards for excellence as a teacher in the area of revolution and is currently preparing a full length study of revolution, entitled, The Revolutionary: A Comparative Study of Communism, Fascism, and Anticolonial Nationalism.

HOW TO ORDER

Papers May Be Purchased Separately. Orders totalling less than $10.00 must be accompanied by payment.

Annual Subscriptions To Twelve Papers Are Available. Professionals and Teachers are offered a one-third discount off the annual institutional rate of $18.00, thus paying only $12.00; FULL-TIME college and university students may subscribe at one-half off the institutional rate—paying only $9.00. Subscription orders at student rates *must* be accompanied by payment.

Clothbound annual volumes of 12 papers are available for the convenience of libraries at $24.00.

Prices Subject to Change Without Notice

ORDER FROM
SAGE PUBLICATIONS, INC. / 275 South Beverly Drive
Beverly Hills, California 90212

If you wish to receive announcements about forthcoming titles in the Sage Professional Papers series, please send your name and address to

SAGE PROFESSIONAL PAPERS
Sage Publications, Inc.
275 S. Beverly Drive
Beverly Hills, California 90212

SAGE PROFESSIONAL PAPERS IN COMPARATIVE POLITICS

VOLUME 1 (1970)

VOLUME 2 (1971)

(Continued on inside back cover)

SAGE Publications / 275 S. Beverly Drive / Beverly Hills, California 90212